The Tw...

Once there were two ogres
who were always fighting.
Each one said that
he had the best magic.

2

"I can be a fire,"
said one. **Zap!**

"I can be water,"
said the other. **Zap!**

3

"I can be a big tree,"
said one. **Zap!**

"I can be a chain saw,"
said the other. **Zap!**

"I can be a spaceship,"
said one. **Zap!**

"I can be a meteor,"
said the other. **Zap!**

5

Then a little girl came by.
She said, "I know
what you cannot be.
You cannot be friends."

6

"What?" cried the ogres.
"Friends? That's easy!"
Zap!

The ogres liked being friends.
They were so happy,
they did not know
that the little girl
had tricked them.

8